A day in the life of an
Astronaut

Contents

Training	2
Morning on the ISS	4
Cooking lunch	6
Eating	8
Cleaning	10
Keeping fit	14
Going to the toilet	16
Rubbish	20
After work	22
Washing	24
Bed time	26
Glossary and index	28
A day on the ISS	30

Written by Mio Debnam

Collins

Training

A career as an **astronaut** is hard work.

You must persevere and spend years training until you can blast off from Earth!

Morning on the ISS

There are three to six **crewmembers** on the ISS. Their main work is research.

8:00 a.m.

They all cook, clear up, repair things and treat sick crewmates, too.

Cooking lunch

Most dishes are first cooked on Earth. On the ISS, liquid is added to the food.

11:45 a.m.

To stop it floating, food is heated in bags.

Eating

Astronauts don't need much gear, like plates, bowls ... or chairs!

12:10 p.m.

They float and eat from the foil cooking bags, or enjoy the food inside a flatbread!

Cleaning

Astronauts can't wash dishes or clothing. They may keep the same clothing on for weeks!

12:50 p.m.

When it needs a wash, clothing has to be thrown away.

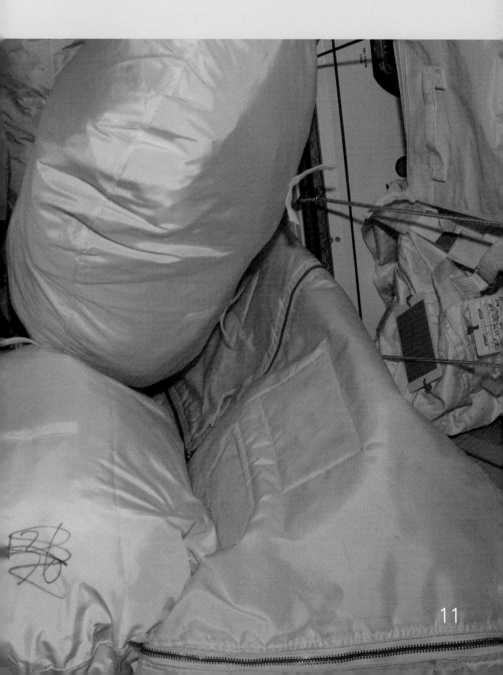

Floating bits of rubbish inside the ship can ruin the **systems** and interfere with experiments, so astronauts clean them up.

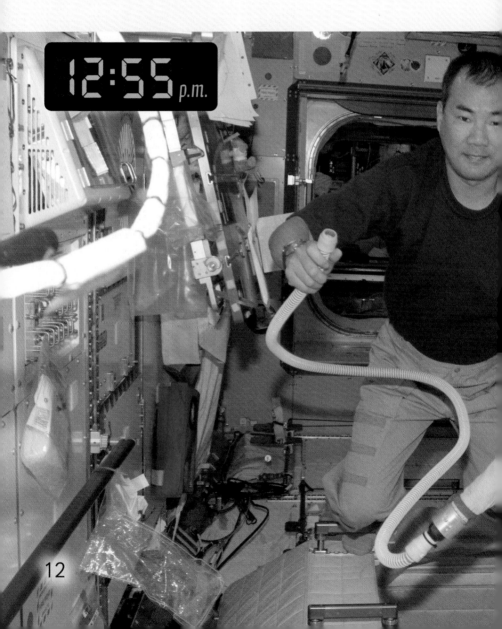

12:55 p.m.

Marks are washed off
with wet wipes.

cleaner

Keeping fit

Astronauts run or **spin** to keep fit.

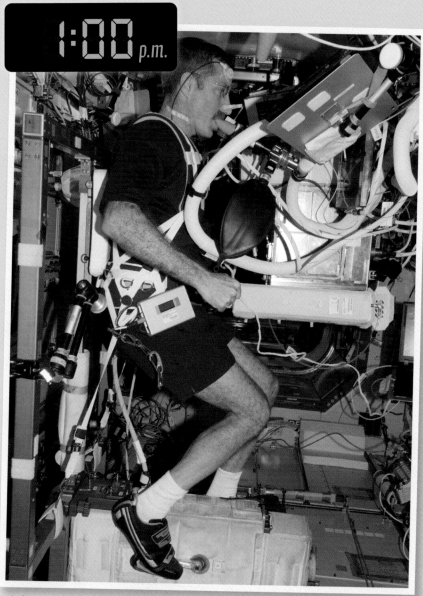

1:00 p.m.

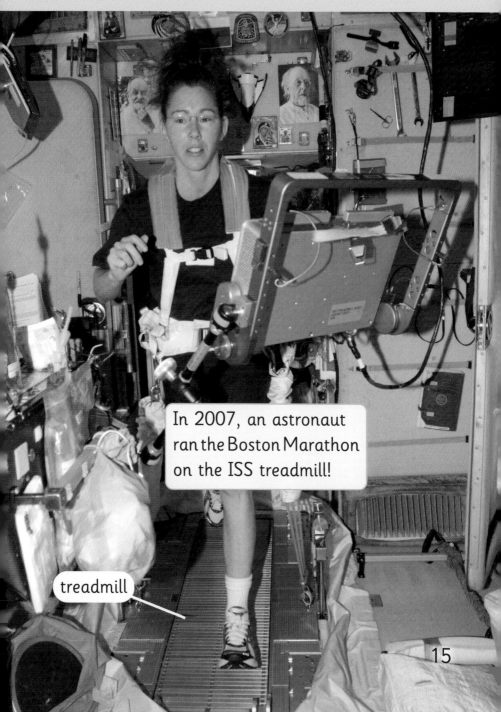

In 2007, an astronaut ran the Boston Marathon on the ISS treadmill!

treadmill

Going to the toilet

The ISS has a toilet that sucks solids into a bag and stops them from floating back up.

2:00 p.m.

The bags are thrown away.

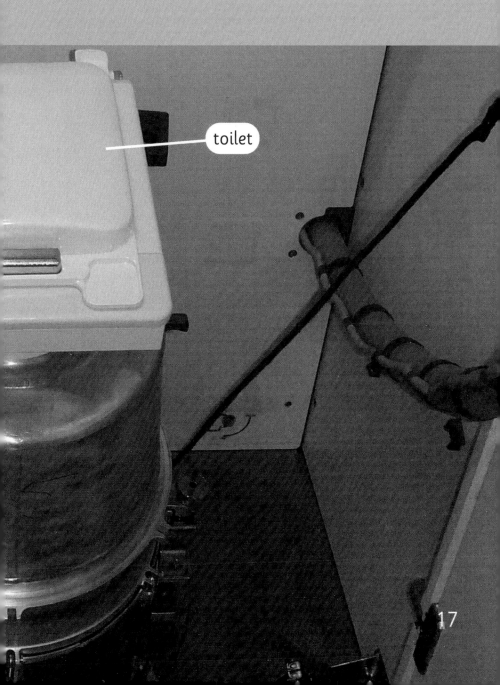

toilet

A hose is used to suck the toilet liquid away.

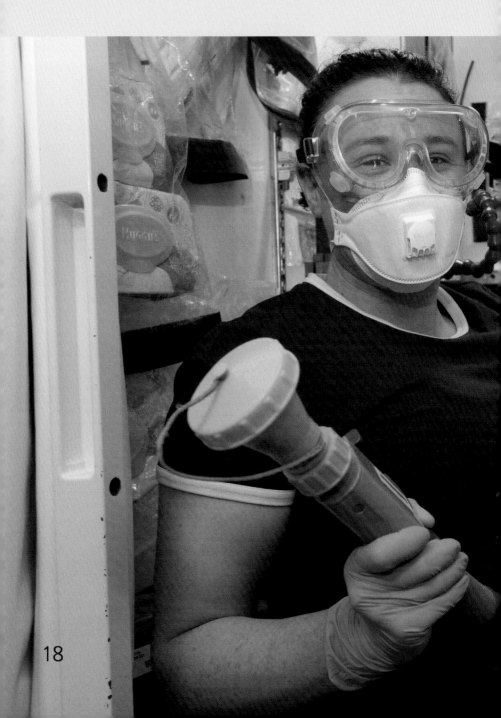

The toilet liquid is collected and turned into clear, clean liquid for drinking, cooking and washing!

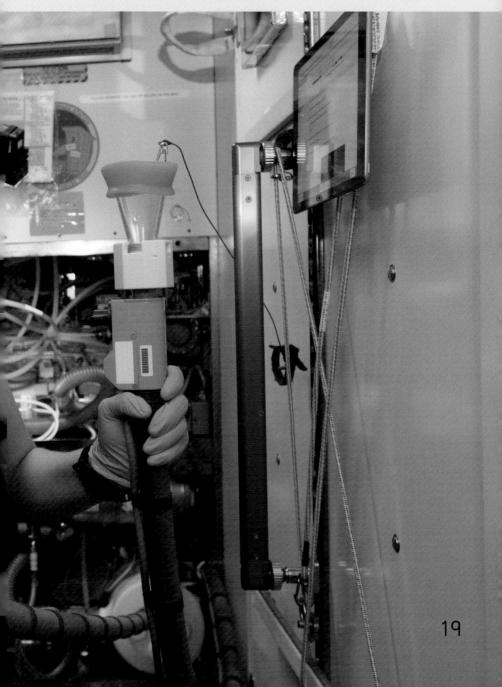

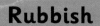

Rubbish

Unmanned rockets deliver things the astronauts need like food, **oxygen** and equipment.

4:50 p.m.

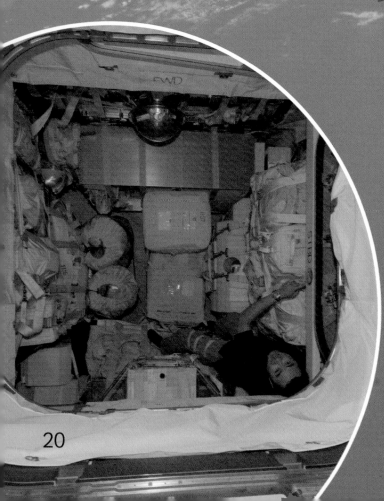

The rockets are then filled with rubbish and sent back. They burn up as they near Earth.

After work

Astronauts read or enjoy a film if they want to relax.

5:00 p.m.

They can use the internet, call their families or peer out at Earth!

Washing

Astronauts wash by squirting on liquid soap or shampoo and wiping with a moist cloth.

8:30 p.m.

By the time they get back to Earth they may stink!

Bed time

This far from Earth, there's no feeling of up or down.

9:30 p.m.

A sleeping bag is attached to the wall of each room to stop astronauts from floating around.

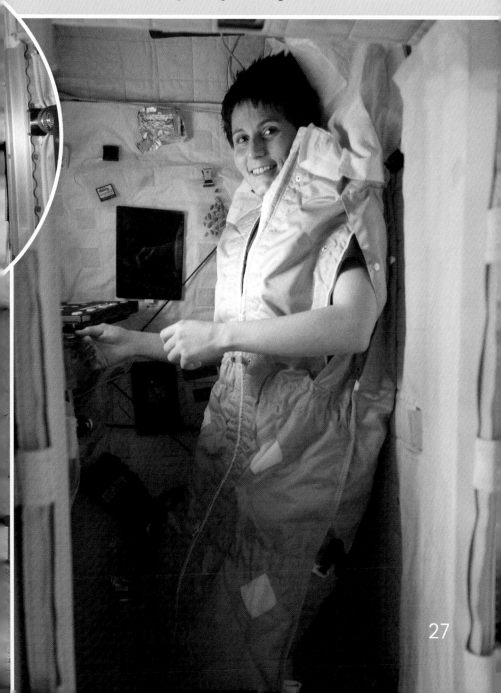

Glossary

astronaut a person trained to work on a rocket or the ISS

crewmembers Three to six astronauts are members of the crew that is on the ISS all the time.

oxygen an important gas we need in order to stay alive

spin use a keep-fit bike

systems the equipment and the computers that control the ISS and the research

unmanned An unmanned rocket has no people on it. It is flown by remote control, using computers.

Index

cleaning 10–11, 12–13

cooking 6–7, 9, 19

cooking bags 9

crewmembers 4–5

food 6–7, 8–9, 20

relaxing 22–23

rubbish 12, 20–21

sleeping bag 27

toilet 16–17, 18–19

training 2–3

treadmill 15

washing 10–11, 19, 24–25

A day on the ISS

8:00 a.m. get up

11:45 a.m. cook lunch

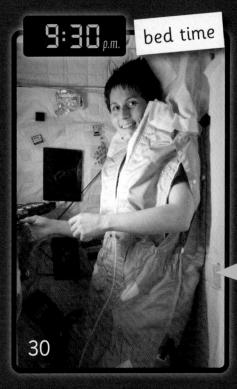

9:30 p.m. bed time

8:30 p.m. wash

12:10 p.m.   eat lunch

12:50 p.m.   clear up

5:00 p.m.   relax

1:00 p.m.   keep fit

After reading

Letters and Sounds: Phase 5

Word count: 378

Focus phonemes: /ai/ ay, a-e, ey /ee/ ie, ea /igh/ i-e, i /oa/ o, ow, o-e /oo/ ew, ou, u, u-e /ar/ a /ow/ ou /or/ al, au /ur/ ear, or, ir /e/ ea /i/ y /ear/ ere, eer /oi/ oy /o/ a

Common exception words: of, to, the, into, by, put, are, be, when, their, there, people, we

Curriculum links: Science: Earth and space

National Curriculum learning objectives: Reading/word reading: read accurately by blending sounds in unfamiliar words containing GPCs that have been taught; read common exception words, noting unusual correspondences between spelling and sound and where these occur in a word; read other words of more than one syllable that contain taught GPCs; Reading/comprehension (KS2): understand what they read, in books they can read independently, by checking that the text makes sense to them, discussing their understanding and explaining the meaning of words in context; identifying main ideas drawn from more than one paragraph and summarising these

Developing fluency

- Take turns to read a double page. Check that your child reads with expression.

Phonic practice

- Ask your child to read the following words and identify the two words that contain /e/ sounds. Which letters make the /e/ sound?
  treadmill (/e/ – ea)   gear   bread (/e/ – ea)   Earth
- Repeat with the following words with the /i/ sound.
  squirting   system (/i/ – y)   wipes   interfere (/i/ – i)

Extending vocabulary

- Challenge your child to explain the meaning of each of the following words and then suggest an antonym (opposite) for each.
  page 3: persevere (e.g. *give up*)   page 7: floating (e.g. *fixed*)
  page 11: thrown away (e.g. *kept*)   page 12: interfere (e.g. *leave alone*)
- Can your child make up a sentence about an astronaut using one of the antonyms?